UNDERSTANDING AUTISM SPECTRUM DISORDER

Comprehensive Guide Key Insights, Behavioral Patterns, Diagnosis, And Support Strategies For All Ages

DR. LINCOLN WAYLON

DISCLAIMER

This book contains information that should only be used for educational and informational reasons; it is not meant to be used as a source of medical or psychological advice. The author's studies, life experiences, and expertise in the area of health and wellness served as the foundation for the content. It should not, however, be used in place of expert counsel, a diagnosis, or medical care.

Any queries you may have about a physical or mental health issue should always be directed toward the advice of a licensed healthcare provider or mental health specialist. With regard to the efficacy or outcomes of the methods or suggestions included in this book, the author and publisher make no representations or warranties.

Any information or methods in this book are used entirely at the reader's own risk and discretion. The material provided here may be used or misused, and neither the author nor the publisher will be held responsible for any results, losses, or negative impacts.

Keep in mind that everyone has different demands and reactions to health and wellness routines. Any health and wellness plans you implement must be customized to your particular circumstances, and you should speak with experts to make sure the plans meet your needs.

TABLE OF CONTENTS

"Understanding Autism Spectrum Disorder" is an essential guide for anyone seeking to grasp the complexities of autism and its impact on individuals and families. This comprehensive resource delves into the fundamental aspects of Autism Spectrum Disorder (ASD), beginning with an overview that provides clarity on the criteria for diagnosing ASD. It offers an in-depth look at common assessment tools and methods, emphasizing the importance of developmental history and observations in preparing for evaluations. By understanding how to interpret these results, readers can better navigate the diagnostic process and make informed decisions about intervention strategies.

The book thoroughly explores the core symptoms and behaviors associated with ASD, including challenges in social communication, repetitive behaviors, restricted interests, and sensory processing differences. Through detailed case studies and examples, it highlights the variability in symptom presentation, offering a nuanced perspective that is crucial for understanding the diverse experiences of those with ASD.

In addressing interventions and therapies, the book provides an overview of evidence-based approaches such as Applied Behavior Analysis (ABA) and speech therapy. It discusses the benefits and limitations of various therapies, guiding readers in selecting the most appropriate options for individual needs. Practical advice on integrating these therapies into daily life, as well as evaluating their progress and effectiveness, is included to support ongoing development and adaptation.

Educational strategies are another focal point, with guidance on creating and implementing Individualized Education Plans (IEPs) and 504 Plans. The book outlines strategies for classroom accommodations, supporting learning and social skills development, and collaborating with educators. It also emphasizes the importance of encouraging self-advocacy within educational settings, empowering individuals with ASD to actively participate in their learning experiences.

Building social skills and relationships is addressed with strategies for improving social interactions, the role of social skills training programs, and ways to encourage peer relationships and social activities. Understanding and managing social anxiety is covered, along with the involvement of family and community in supporting social skill development.

Sensory sensitivities are examined with practical strategies for managing sensory overload and creating sensory-friendly environments at home and school. The book also discusses the use of sensory integration therapy and advocacy for sensory needs in public settings.

Support for mental health and well-being is a key component, focusing on common co-occurring issues such as anxiety and depression. It offers strategies for emotional regulation, the importance of routine and structure, and building resilience and self-esteem.

Access to mental health support and resources is also highlighted.

Navigating family dynamics is addressed by exploring the impact of ASD on family relationships and providing coping strategies for parents and siblings. The book offers guidance on finding support groups, balancing caregiving with personal well-being, and strengthening family communication and unity.

Looking toward the future, the book discusses transitioning to adulthood and independent living, including employment and vocational training opportunities, financial planning, legal considerations, and community resources. Long-term goals and life planning are also considered, providing a roadmap for future success.

The book presents a wealth of resources and advocacy information, including national and local autism organizations, online communities, and guidance on advocating for better services and policies. It also covers finding and utilizing funding and grants and staying informed about ongoing research and developments in the field of ASD.

Common concerns such as recognizing the need for a diagnosis, handling disagreements with professional assessments, effectively communicating a child's needs, supporting therapy sessions, and managing the stress of caregiving are also addressed, ensuring that readers have a comprehensive and supportive guide to understanding and managing Autism Spectrum Disorder.

CHAPTER ONE

OVERVIEW OF AUTISM SPECTRUM DISORDER

CRITERIA FOR DIAGNOSING ASD

Diagnosing Autism Spectrum Disorder (ASD) involves a comprehensive assessment based on a set of established criteria. The primary criteria used are outlined in the Diagnostic and Statistical Manual of Mental Disorders, Fifth Edition (DSM-5), which includes persistent deficits in social communication and interaction across multiple contexts. This is coupled with restricted, repetitive patterns of behavior, interests, or activities. Clinicians observe these behaviors across different settings and times to ensure consistency and severity, meeting the DSM-5 thresholds. The diagnosis often requires evidence of these symptoms being present from early childhood, even if they are not fully recognized until later.

To accurately diagnose ASD, the clinical evaluation includes both direct observation and parent/caregiver interviews. Health professionals assess developmental milestones, communication skills, and social interactions. They look for specific behaviors such as repetitive movements, fixation on particular topics, or challenges with change and transitions.

The evaluation often incorporates standardized tools and checklists to quantify these behaviors and compare them with typical developmental patterns. This approach helps in identifying ASD traits and ruling out other conditions that might present with similar symptoms.

The diagnosis is not based on a single test but rather a combination of assessments that consider the child's overall developmental history and current functioning. The clinical team will evaluate the child's behavior in structured and natural settings, seeking patterns that align with ASD criteria. This thorough process ensures a precise diagnosis, which is critical for planning effective interventions and support strategies.

Understanding these criteria helps in recognizing early signs of ASD and seeking timely professional evaluation.

COMMON ASSESSMENT TOOLS AND METHODS

Various assessment tools and methods are utilized to evaluate and diagnose Autism Spectrum Disorder. One of the most widely used tools is the Autism Diagnostic Observation Schedule (ADOS), which provides a structured interaction to observe behaviors directly. ADOS involve standardized activities and scenarios that elicit responses relevant to social communication, play, and repetitive behaviors, allowing clinicians to assess ASD symptoms in a controlled environment. Another significant tool is the Autism Diagnostic Interview-Revised (ADI-R), which involves detailed interviews with caregivers about the child's developmental history and behaviors.

In addition to these tools, the Childhood Autism Rating Scale (CARS) is used to rate behaviors on a scale from mild to severe, providing a quantitative measure of the severity of ASD symptoms. The Social Communication Questionnaire (SCQ) is another screening tool that helps identify potential ASD by evaluating social communication skills and behaviors. These tools are often complemented by developmental checklists and behavioral questionnaires that provide a comprehensive view of the child's functioning.

The use of these tools is combined with clinical judgment to ensure a holistic assessment. The integration of multiple methods helps validate the findings and provides a clearer picture of the child's developmental profile.

Clinicians may also use observational assessments and parent reports to supplement formal tools, ensuring that the evaluation captures all relevant aspects of the child's behavior and developmental history.

THE ROLE OF DEVELOPMENTAL HISTORY AND OBSERVATIONS

Developmental history and observations are critical components in diagnosing Autism Spectrum Disorder. The developmental history provides context about the child's early milestones, including speech, motor skills, and social interactions.

This history is gathered through detailed interviews with parents or caregivers, who provide insights into how the child has progressed over time and any concerns they may have had. This background helps clinicians understand whether the behaviors observed are consistent with ASD or if they might be indicative of other developmental issues.

Observations play a vital role in the assessment process, as they offer direct insight into how the child interacts with their environment and other people. Clinicians observe the child's behavior in various settings to identify patterns of social interaction, communication, and repetitive behaviors.

These observations help determine whether the child's behaviors align with the diagnostic criteria for ASD. Observing how a child responds to different stimuli and interactions provides valuable information about their social and communication skills.

Combining developmental history with observational data allows clinicians to assess the consistency of the child's behaviors over time and in different contexts. This comprehensive approach ensures that the diagnosis of ASD is based on a thorough understanding of the child's developmental trajectory and current functioning.

It also helps in distinguishing ASD from other conditions that may present with similar symptoms but have different developmental patterns.

HOW TO PREPARE FOR EVALUATIONS

Preparing for evaluations for Autism Spectrum Disorder involves several key steps to ensure a smooth and effective assessment process. First, gathering relevant information about the child's developmental history and behavioral patterns is crucial.

Parents or caregivers should compile records of milestones, previous evaluations, and any concerns they have about the child's development. This information provides a comprehensive background that will be helpful during the assessment and ensures that the evaluation is informed by a complete picture of the child's history.

Next, it's essential to familiarize oneself with the assessment process and tools that will be used. Understanding what to expect during the evaluation can help reduce anxiety and ensure that the process goes smoothly.

Parents or caregivers should prepare to answer questions about the child's behavior, routines, and developmental history. It may also be helpful to review any questionnaires or checklists that will be used during the assessment to provide accurate and detailed responses.

Finally, ensuring that the child is comfortable and prepared for the evaluation is important. This may involve explaining the process in an age-appropriate way and helping the child understand that the evaluation is a normal part of learning about their needs. Preparing the child emotionally and practically can help them feel more at ease and allow the assessment to proceed without unnecessary stress. By taking these preparatory steps, parents and caregivers can facilitate a more effective and comprehensive evaluation.

UNDERSTANDING AND INTERPRETING RESULTS

Understanding and interpreting the results of an Autism Spectrum Disorder evaluation involves analyzing the data gathered from various assessments and observations. The results are typically presented in the form of reports that include findings from diagnostic tools, behavioral observations, and developmental history. It is crucial to review these results with a clinician who can explain how they align with the diagnostic criteria for ASD and what they indicate about the child's strengths and challenges.

Interpreting results involves looking at how the child's behaviors and developmental patterns compare to established benchmarks for ASD. Clinicians will discuss the significance of specific findings, such as difficulties in social communication or repetitive behaviors, and how these fit into the overall diagnostic picture.

Understanding the results also involves recognizing that ASD is a spectrum, meaning that each child's presentation may vary widely, and the diagnosis is tailored to their individual needs.

Finally, the results of the evaluation are used to develop a tailored intervention plan. This plan outlines specific strategies and supports that can address the child's unique needs and promote their development. By understanding the results, parents and caregivers can work with professionals to implement effective interventions and monitor progress. This collaborative approach ensures that the child receives the appropriate support and resources to thrive.

CHAPTER TWO

CORE SYMPTOMS AND BEHAVIORS

SOCIAL COMMUNICATION CHALLENGES

Social communication challenges are a core aspect of Autism Spectrum Disorder (ASD), manifesting in difficulties with verbal and non-verbal communication. Individuals may struggle with initiating and maintaining conversations, interpreting social cues, and understanding the subtleties of body language or facial expressions. This often results in a communication style that may appear unusual to others, such as taking language literally or having trouble grasping implied meanings or sarcasm.

To support individuals with ASD in improving social communication, it is essential to employ strategies such as social skills training and tailored communication interventions. These may include role-playing exercises to practice conversational skills, using visual aids to clarify social rules, and employing clear, direct language. Support can also come from specialized therapies that focus on enhancing both verbal and non-verbal communication skills, helping individuals navigate social interactions more effectively.

Practical approaches for addressing social communication challenges include creating structured social environments where individuals can practice skills in a controlled setting. Implementing peer modeling, where individuals with ASD observe and learn from others, can be beneficial. Additionally, encouraging consistent routines and clear expectations in social contexts can help reduce anxiety and improve overall communication effectiveness.

REPETITIVE BEHAVIORS AND RESTRICTED INTERESTS

Repetitive behaviors and restricted interests are hallmark characteristics of ASD, often involving a strong focus on specific activities or routines. Individuals may engage in repetitive actions, such as hand-flapping or rocking, or become intensely interested in narrow topics, such as train schedules or specific types of machinery. These behaviors can serve as coping mechanisms or a way to find comfort and predictability in their environment.

To manage and understand these behaviors, it is important to recognize their role in providing a sense of security and predictability. Developing coping strategies, such as introducing alternative, acceptable repetitive activities or gradually broadening interests through structured activities, can help individuals manage these tendencies without disrupting daily life. Therapeutic interventions, including cognitive-behavioral therapy (CBT), can also be useful in addressing the underlying needs that these behaviors may signify.

Encouraging flexibility within structured routines and gradually introducing new activities can help individuals expand their interests. Positive reinforcement for engaging in new experiences and allowing choices in activities can foster a more balanced approach to managing repetitive behaviors. Additionally, creating a supportive environment that acknowledges and accommodates these behaviors while gently encouraging diversification can help maintain overall well-being.

SENSORY PROCESSING DIFFERENCES

Sensory processing differences in ASD involve heightened or diminished responses to sensory stimuli, such as sounds, lights, textures, or smells. Individuals may experience sensory overload or seek out certain sensory experiences to a greater degree than those without ASD. This can lead to challenges in environments where sensory inputs are unpredictable or overwhelming, affecting daily functioning and comfort.

To address sensory processing differences, it is crucial to identify specific sensory triggers and develop strategies to manage them effectively. This might include creating sensory-friendly spaces with reduced stimuli or providing sensory tools, such as noise-canceling headphones or textured fidget toys. Implementing sensory diets, which consist of planned activities to meet sensory needs, can also be beneficial in helping individuals self-regulate and adapt to their environments.

Creating an accommodating environment involves understanding individual sensory preferences and sensitivities. For instance, adjusting lighting, reducing background noise, or providing options for sensory breaks can significantly enhance comfort and focus. By tailoring environmental adjustments and sensory supports to the individual's needs, it is possible to create more manageable and enjoyable experiences.

VARIABILITY IN SYMPTOM PRESENTATION

ASD presents with a high degree of variability in symptom presentation, meaning that no two individuals with ASD exhibit the same set of characteristics or intensity of symptoms.

This variability can include differences in communication abilities, social interactions, cognitive skills, and behavioral patterns. Understanding this variability is crucial for providing effective, individualized support.

Assessing and supporting individuals with ASD requires a personalized approach that considers their unique strengths and challenges. This involves conducting thorough assessments to identify specific needs and tailoring interventions accordingly. For example, some individuals may benefit from more intensive behavioral therapies, while others may require support in developing communication skills or managing sensory sensitivities.

By recognizing the spectrum of symptoms and customizing strategies to fit individual profiles, caregivers and professionals can provide more effective support. Adapting interventions and support systems to the specific manifestations of ASD in each person ensures that their unique needs are met, promoting better outcomes and overall quality of life.

CASE STUDIES AND EXAMPLES

Case studies and examples offer valuable insights into how ASD manifests and how various interventions can be implemented effectively. For instance, a case study involving a child with ASD who has difficulty with social interactions might illustrate how targeted social skills training and peer interactions improve their ability to engage in group activities. Another example might showcase an adult with ASD who benefits from structured routines and sensory accommodations in their workplace.

Examining real-life examples helps to understand how theoretical concepts and interventions are applied in practice. These case studies often highlight successful strategies and areas for improvement, providing practical guidance for managing similar challenges. They also offer a glimpse into the diverse experiences of individuals with ASD, showcasing the range of interventions and supports that can be beneficial.

By studying these examples, caregivers and professionals can gain a better understanding of how to tailor interventions to meet the specific needs of individuals with ASD. Insights from case studies can inform best practices, guide decision-making, and inspire innovative approaches to supporting individuals on the autism spectrum.

CHAPTER THREE

INTERVENTIONS AND THERAPIES

OVERVIEW OF EVIDENCE-BASED THERAPIES

Evidence-based therapies are crucial in supporting individuals with Autism Spectrum Disorder (ASD). Applied Behavior Analysis (ABA) is a widely used approach that focuses on reinforcing desired behaviors and reducing unwanted ones through systematic interventions.

ABA involves breaking down complex skills into smaller, manageable tasks and using positive reinforcement to encourage progress. Speech therapy, on the other hand, targets communication challenges by developing language skills, improving articulation, and enhancing social communication abilities.

These therapies are grounded in research and have shown effectiveness in improving various aspects of functioning in individuals with ASD.

Other evidence-based therapies include occupational therapy, which helps individuals develop daily living skills and sensory processing abilities, and social skills training, which aims to improve interpersonal interactions and social understanding. Each therapy employs specific techniques and strategies designed to address the unique needs of individuals with ASD, offering a tailored approach to enhance their quality of life. By utilizing these evidence-based therapies, practitioners can provide targeted support that aligns with the latest research and best practices.

BENEFITS AND LIMITATIONS OF DIFFERENT APPROACHES

ABA therapy offers significant benefits, such as its structured approach and measurable outcomes. It has been shown to improve various skills, including communication, social interactions, and adaptive behavior. However, ABA can be intensive and may require a significant time commitment, which can be challenging for some families.

Speech therapy also provides notable benefits, such as enhancing verbal communication and social interaction skills, but its effectiveness can vary depending on the individual's specific needs and goals.

Occupational therapy helps with sensory integration and daily living skills, which can significantly impact an individual's ability to function independently. Yet, the results might be gradual and require patience and consistency. Social skills training fosters improved interpersonal relationships, but the generalization of these skills to real-world settings can be a limitation. Each therapy has its strengths and potential drawbacks, making it essential to consider these factors when selecting the most appropriate approach for an individual with ASD.

HOW TO CHOOSE THE RIGHT THERAPY FOR YOUR NEEDS

Choosing the right therapy for an individual with ASD involves assessing their unique strengths and challenges. Start by evaluating the specific areas where the individual needs support, such as communication, social skills, or daily living activities. Consulting with professionals, such as a developmental pediatrician or a clinical psychologist, can provide valuable insights into which therapy may be most beneficial. Additionally, consider the individual's preferences and interests, as engaging in therapy that aligns with their natural inclinations can enhance motivation and participation.

It's also important to review the qualifications and experience of therapists to ensure they are well-versed in working with individuals with ASD. Research various therapy programs and their evidence base to determine which ones have demonstrated effectiveness in addressing similar needs.

Integrating therapies into daily life is essential for maximizing their effectiveness and ensuring that skills learned in therapy are applied in real-world situations. For instance, ABA techniques can be used throughout the day by incorporating behavior management strategies into everyday routines. Consistency in applying these techniques at home and in community settings reinforces the skills being developed. Speech therapy practices, such as communication exercises, can be incorporated into family interactions and daily conversations to enhance language use in natural contexts.

Occupational therapy techniques, such as sensory activities or adaptive strategies, should be integrated into daily routines to improve sensory processing and daily living skills. Social skills training can be practiced during family activities or social interactions to generalize skills learned in therapy. By embedding therapeutic techniques into everyday activities, individuals with ASD can better transfer skills from therapy to real-life scenarios, leading to more meaningful and sustained progress.

EVALUATING THERAPY PROGRESS AND EFFECTIVENESS

Evaluating therapy progress and effectiveness involves monitoring the individual's development and making adjustments as needed. Regular assessments by the therapist can track improvements in targeted areas, such as communication, behavior, or daily living skills. It's crucial to set specific, measurable goals and periodically review them to assess whether the therapy is meeting the desired outcomes. Engaging in open communication with the therapist about progress and any challenges encountered ensures that the therapy can be adapted to better suit the individual's evolving needs.

Parents and caregivers should also be involved in the evaluation process by documenting observations and changes in behavior or skills. Keeping detailed records of therapy sessions and their impact on daily life can provide valuable insights into the therapy's effectiveness.

CHAPTER FOUR

EDUCATIONAL STRATEGIES FOR ASD

INDIVIDUALIZED EDUCATION PLANS (IEPS) AND 504 PLANS

Individualized Education Plans (IEPs) are customized educational plans developed for students with special needs under the Individuals with Disabilities Education Act (IDEA). An IEP is tailored to address the specific educational requirements of a student diagnosed with Autism Spectrum Disorder (ASD). It outlines specific learning goals, the services and support needed, and how progress will be measured. To create an effective IEP, a team including teachers, parents, and sometimes the student, collaborates to set goals and determine the necessary supports, such as specialized instruction or therapy. Each IEP is unique and reviewed annually to ensure it meets the student's evolving needs.

A 504 Plan, named after Section 504 of the Rehabilitation Act, provides accommodations for students with disabilities to ensure they have equal access to education. Unlike IEPs, 504 Plans do not focus on specialized instruction but on adjustments that allow students to participate in the general education curriculum.

These plans might include accommodations like extended test time, preferential seating, or the use of assistive technology. Developing a 504 Plan involves a process where educators and parents discuss the student's needs and determine appropriate modifications, ensuring the student can access the same educational opportunities as their peers.

For both IEPs and 504 Plans, collaboration between parents, educators, and specialists is key. Parents should advocate for their child's needs, ensuring that the plans are reviewed and adjusted as necessary.

Regular meetings and open communication help in monitoring the student's progress and making adjustments to the plans. The goal is to provide a supportive educational environment that addresses the unique challenges faced by students with ASD and helps them succeed academically and socially.

CLASSROOM ACCOMMODATIONS AND MODIFICATIONS

Classroom accommodations and modifications are strategies used to adapt the learning environment to meet the needs of students with ASD. Accommodations might include changes in the classroom setup, such as providing a quiet space for students who need it or using visual schedules to help them understand daily routines. Modifications, on the other hand, involve altering the curriculum or assignments to better suit the student's learning needs. For instance, breaking tasks into smaller steps or using alternative methods for assessments can help students with ASD engage more effectively in their learning.

To implement these strategies, teachers and support staff must first identify the specific needs of the student through observations and assessments.

They then tailor accommodations and modifications to those needs, ensuring they are practical and beneficial. For example, a student who has difficulty with written assignments might benefit from oral presentations or the use of speech-to-text software. Consistent implementation and adjustment of these strategies are crucial for maximizing their effectiveness and supporting the student's educational progress.

Collaboration with parents and other professionals is essential in developing and refining accommodations and modifications. Teachers should regularly review and adjust these strategies based on the student's progress and feedback. Engaging the students in discussions about what works best for them can also provide valuable insights.

SUPPORTING LEARNING AND SOCIAL SKILLS DEVELOPMENT

Supporting learning and social skills development for students with ASD involves targeted strategies to enhance their ability to interact and engage in educational settings. This includes implementing structured social skills training programs that teach appropriate behaviors, communication techniques, and ways to build relationships with peers. Programs might use role-playing, social stories, or peer mentoring to practice these skills in a controlled and supportive environment. Regular practice and reinforcement in various social settings help students generalize these skills and apply them in real-life situations.

In addition to social skills training, academic support is crucial. Teachers can use visual aids, hands-on activities, and step-by-step instructions to make learning more accessible. Breaking down complex tasks into smaller, manageable parts and using positive reinforcement can motivate students and help them achieve their educational goals. Creating a supportive and inclusive classroom atmosphere where students with ASD feel safe and valued is essential for their learning and social development.

Parents and educators should work together to create consistent strategies both at home and school. This collaboration ensures that social skills and academic strategies are reinforced across different settings, providing a unified approach to the student's development. Regular monitoring and feedback help in adjusting strategies to better meet the student's evolving needs and in celebrating their successes, fostering their growth and confidence.

WORKING WITH EDUCATORS AND SCHOOL STAFF

Effective collaboration with educators and school staff is vital for supporting students with ASD. Building strong relationships with teachers and staff helps ensure that the student's needs are understood and addressed. Regular communication between parents and school personnel allows for the sharing of observations, strategies, and updates on the student's progress. Parents need to advocate for their children's needs while also being open to feedback and suggestions from educators.

Teachers and school staff can benefit from training and professional development focused on understanding and supporting students with ASD. This training can provide educators with strategies for managing classroom behavior, creating inclusive learning environments, and implementing individualized instruction. Establishing a team approach where everyone involved in the student's education is informed and aligned with the student's goals enhances the effectiveness of support strategies.

Parent-teacher conferences and regular meetings are opportunities to discuss the student's progress, review the effectiveness of accommodations and modifications, and plan for future needs.

ENCOURAGING SELF-ADVOCACY IN EDUCATIONAL SETTINGS

Encouraging self-advocacy involves teaching students with ASD to understand and communicate their needs, preferences, and rights within the educational environment.

Self-advocacy skills empower students to take an active role in their education by expressing what accommodations or supports they require and participating in decision-making processes regarding their learning. This can include teaching them how to ask for help, explain their learning preferences, and articulate their goals and challenges.

Strategies to promote self-advocacy include providing opportunities for students to practice these skills in a supportive setting, such as role-playing scenarios or guided discussions. Educators can help by involving students in their IEP or 504 Plan meetings, encouraging them to voice their opinions and preferences. Additionally, providing students with resources and tools, such as self-advocacy checklists or visual aids, can help them better manage their needs and navigate their educational experience.

Parents play a crucial role in supporting their child's development of self-advocacy skills by reinforcing these strategies at home and encouraging their child to take an active role in their educational journey.

CHAPTER FIVE

BUILDING SOCIAL SKILLS AND RELATIONSHIPS

STRATEGIES FOR IMPROVING SOCIAL INTERACTIONS

Improving social interactions for individuals with Autism Spectrum Disorder (ASD) involves implementing practical strategies tailored to their unique needs. One effective approach is using visual supports, such as social stories and pictorial schedules, to help individuals understand and navigate social situations. Visual aids can provide clear, step-by-step instructions and expectations, reducing confusion and anxiety in social settings. For example, a visual schedule might outline the steps for starting a conversation, including greeting, making eye contact, and taking turns speaking.

Another important strategy is role-playing exercises, which allow individuals to practice social scenarios in a controlled environment. Role-playing can help them rehearse appropriate responses and develop confidence in various social interactions. For instance, practicing how to ask a peer to join a game or how to respond to a compliment can make these situations more manageable and less intimidating. Additionally, using structured playdates or social groups with specific goals and routines can further enhance these skills by providing consistent practice opportunities.

Finally, providing positive reinforcement for successful social interactions can motivate individuals with ASD to continue developing their social skills. Recognizing and celebrating small achievements, such as initiating a conversation or making a new friend, helps build self-esteem and encourages further progress. Using verbal praise, rewards, or tokens can reinforce desired behaviors and make social interactions more enjoyable and less stressful.

ROLE OF SOCIAL SKILLS TRAINING PROGRAMS

Social skills training programs play a crucial role in helping individuals with ASD develop effective communication and interaction abilities. These programs typically involve structured lessons that focus on specific social skills, such as making eye contact, understanding body language, and engaging in reciprocal conversations. They often use techniques like modeling, role-playing, and video feedback to teach and reinforce these skills in a supportive environment.

Programs are usually tailored to meet the needs of different age groups and skill levels, offering a range of activities designed to address various social challenges. For younger children, activities might include simple turn-taking games and basic conversation practice, while older individuals may engage in more complex scenarios, such as navigating social hierarchies or managing conflicts. The use of evidence-based approaches and ongoing assessment helps ensure that the training remains effective and relevant to each participant's needs.

Additionally, many social skills training programs involve collaboration with families and educators to support the generalization of skills outside of the program. By integrating training into everyday routines and providing guidance on how to reinforce skills at home and in school, these programs help individuals with ASD transfer their learning to real-world situations, enhancing their overall social functioning.

ENCOURAGING PEER RELATIONSHIPS AND SOCIAL ACTIVITIES

Encouraging peer relationships and participation in social activities is essential for the social development of individuals with ASD. Creating opportunities for social engagement, such as joining clubs, teams, or interest-based groups, can help individuals connect with peers who share similar interests.

 For example, a child interested in art might benefit from joining an art class where they can meet others with a shared passion, facilitating natural social interactions and friendships.

Structured social activities, like group outings or organized playdates, provide a safe and predictable environment for individuals with ASD to practice social skills and build relationships. These activities can be tailored to the individual's preferences and comfort levels, ensuring that they are engaging and enjoyable. For instance, a small group game or craft session can offer a relaxed setting for practicing turn-taking, communication, and cooperation.

Fostering an inclusive environment where peers are educated about ASD and encouraged to interact with their classmates or friends with the condition can also enhance social integration. Schools and community programs that promote understanding and empathy among peers help reduce stigma and create supportive networks, making it easier for individuals with ASD to form meaningful connections.

UNDERSTANDING AND MANAGING SOCIAL ANXIETY

Social anxiety is a common challenge for individuals with ASD, often exacerbated by unfamiliar social situations or perceived social expectations. Understanding the specific triggers and manifestations of social anxiety in individuals with ASD is crucial for effective management. For example, recognizing signs of anxiety, such as avoidance behaviors or physical symptoms like sweating or trembling, can help in tailoring interventions to address these concerns.

Cognitive-behavioral strategies can be beneficial in managing social anxiety. Techniques such as gradual exposure to feared social situations, relaxation exercises, and cognitive restructuring can help individuals learn to cope with anxiety and reduce its impact. For instance, starting with less intimidating social scenarios and gradually increasing the complexity can help build confidence and reduce anxiety over time.

Involving a therapist or counselor who specializes in anxiety management and ASD can provide additional support. These professionals can offer personalized strategies and interventions to address specific anxieties and develop coping skills. Regular sessions and collaborative work with families can ensure that strategies are effectively implemented and adapted to the individual's evolving needs.

INVOLVING FAMILY AND COMMUNITY IN SOCIAL SKILL DEVELOPMENT

The involvement of family and community is crucial in supporting the social skill development of individuals with ASD. Families play a key role in reinforcing social skills learned in therapy or training programs by incorporating these skills into daily routines and interactions. For example, practicing conversational skills during family meals or involving family members in role-playing activities can help reinforce learning and provide real-life practice opportunities.

Community involvement, such as participation in local groups, clubs, or events, offers additional support and practice for social skills. Creating inclusive environments where individuals with ASD are welcomed and supported helps facilitate their social development. Community organizations can provide valuable resources, social activities, and peer interactions that enhance social skill acquisition and integration.

Collaborating with educators, therapists, and community leaders ensures a consistent approach to social skill development. By sharing information, strategies, and progress updates, families can work together with professionals and community members to create a cohesive support system that fosters social growth and inclusion for individuals with ASD.

CHAPTER SIX

ADDRESSING SENSORY SENSITIVITIES

COMMON SENSORY ISSUES IN ASD

Individuals with Autism Spectrum Disorder (ASD) often experience heightened or diminished responses to sensory stimuli. Common sensory issues include hypersensitivity, where everyday sounds, lights, or textures can feel overwhelming or painful.

 For instance, the hum of fluorescent light or the texture of certain fabrics may be intolerable for those affected. Conversely, some individuals might have hyposensitivity, requiring stronger stimuli to register, such as seeking out intense sensory experiences like loud noises or rough textures to feel engaged.

Understanding these sensory issues involves recognizing the diverse ways individuals with ASD perceive their environment. For example, a person might react strongly to the smell of certain foods or become distressed by the visual clutter in a room. Identifying specific triggers can help tailor interventions to manage these sensitivities effectively, enhancing the individual's comfort and quality of life.

Addressing these sensory challenges requires both awareness and accommodation. By carefully observing and documenting sensory responses, caregivers and educators can better understand the unique needs of each individual.

This approach enables the development of personalized strategies to minimize discomfort and support more positive sensory experiences.

STRATEGIES FOR MANAGING SENSORY OVERLOAD

Managing sensory overload involves several proactive strategies aimed at reducing the impact of overwhelming stimuli. One effective method is implementing sensory breaks, which provide a quiet space where individuals can retreat and recover from sensory input. Creating a calming environment with soft lighting, noise-canceling headphones, or weighted blankets can help individuals regain their composure and reduce anxiety.

Another strategy is to use sensory modulation techniques, such as engaging in activities that offer soothing or stimulating experiences tailored to the individual's needs. For instance, using stress balls or sensory mats can provide a tactile focus, while listening to calming music or practicing deep-breathing exercises can help alleviate sensory overload. Establishing a routine that includes regular sensory breaks and activities can also help manage sensory sensitivities effectively.

Educators and caregivers can collaborate to identify potential triggers and adjust the environment accordingly. This might involve reducing unnecessary noise, adjusting lighting, or incorporating sensory-friendly tools into daily routines. By creating a supportive and adaptable environment, individuals with ASD can better navigate sensory challenges and improve their overall well-being.

CREATING A SENSORY-FRIENDLY ENVIRONMENT AT HOME AND SCHOOL

Creating a sensory-friendly environment involves modifying spaces to cater to the sensory needs of individuals with ASD. At home, this might mean setting up a designated quiet area where the individual can escape from overstimulating situations. Using soft, calming colors for walls, and minimizing clutter can help create a serene atmosphere. Additionally, incorporating sensory-friendly furniture like bean bags or cushioned chairs can enhance comfort.

In educational settings, it's essential to consider the sensory needs of students when designing classroom environments. This might involve providing noise-canceling headphones, adjustable lighting, or sensory tools such as fidget toys. Teachers can also establish quiet zones within the classroom where students can go when feeling overwhelmed, ensuring that these areas are easily accessible and equipped with calming resources.

Adjustments to daily routines and classroom activities can also support sensory needs. For example, incorporating sensory breaks into the schedule, allowing flexible seating arrangements, and using visual schedules can help manage sensory overload and enhance focus. By thoughtfully designing both home and school environments, individuals with ASD can experience a more comfortable and supportive atmosphere conducive to their well-being.

USING SENSORY INTEGRATION THERAPY

Sensory integration therapy aims to help individuals with ASD better process and respond to sensory information. This therapy involves structured activities designed to improve sensory processing skills and help individuals adapt to sensory stimuli more effectively. For instance, activities such as swinging, spinning, or playing with textured materials can help improve sensory integration and coordination.

Therapists often use a variety of techniques tailored to the individual's specific sensory needs. These may include proprioceptive activities, which involve activities that provide feedback from muscles and joints, or vestibular activities, which involve movement and balance.

By engaging in these activities, individuals can develop better sensory processing skills and increase their tolerance to sensory experiences.

Regular sessions with a trained occupational therapist can guide individuals through sensory integration therapy, helping them build coping strategies and improve their overall sensory processing.

The goal is to create a more balanced sensory experience, allowing individuals to function more comfortably in daily activities and environments.

ADVOCATING FOR SENSORY NEEDS IN PUBLIC SETTINGS

Advocating for sensory needs in public settings involves raising awareness and promoting accommodations that support individuals with ASD. This can include requesting modifications to public spaces, such as providing quiet areas in airports or public transport, and ensuring that events and facilities are designed with sensory-friendly features. Effective advocacy often involves working with organizations and public officials to implement these changes.

In everyday situations, individuals and their caregivers can use various tools to communicate sensory needs.

For instance, carrying a sensory needs card or using apps that help explain sensory preferences can facilitate communication with staff and service providers?

These tools can help ensure that specific accommodations are made, such as adjusting lighting or reducing noise levels in public spaces.

Building partnerships with advocacy groups and participating in community efforts can further support sensory needs in public settings. By collaborating with others who share similar goals and engaging in local initiatives, individuals can contribute to broader changes that benefit the autism community. Advocacy efforts can help create more inclusive environments, enhancing the overall quality of life for those with sensory sensitivities.

CHAPTER SEVEN

SUPPORTING MENTAL HEALTH AND WELL-BEING

COMMON CO-OCCURRING MENTAL HEALTH ISSUES

Autism Spectrum Disorder (ASD) often coexists with other mental health challenges, such as anxiety and depression. Individuals with ASD may experience heightened anxiety due to sensory sensitivities, social interactions, or changes in routine. Depression can also occur, particularly if there are struggles with social integration or feelings of isolation. Recognizing these co-occurring conditions is crucial for providing comprehensive support. Caregivers and professionals need to monitor signs of anxiety and depression, such as changes in behavior, mood swings, or withdrawal from activities.

Addressing these co-occurring issues involves a multi-faceted approach. Therapy options like Cognitive Behavioral Therapy (CBT) can be tailored to help manage anxiety and depressive symptoms. Additionally, medications may be prescribed to alleviate severe symptoms, but these should be managed by a healthcare professional. Creating a supportive environment that acknowledges and addresses these mental health challenges is key.

This includes ensuring access to mental health professionals who understand the unique needs of individuals with ASD.

To support individuals with ASD dealing with co-occurring mental health issues, it's important to foster open communication and encourage them to express their feelings.

Providing a safe space where they can talk about their concerns without judgment can help in early identification and intervention. Integrating mental health support into their routine can make a significant difference in managing these conditions effectively.

STRATEGIES FOR EMOTIONAL REGULATION AND COPING

Emotional regulation and coping strategies are vital for individuals with ASD to manage their emotions effectively. Techniques such as mindfulness and relaxation exercises can help in managing stress and anxiety. Teaching deep-breathing exercises or progressive muscle relaxation can provide individuals with tools to calm themselves during moments of emotional upheaval. Incorporating these strategies into daily routines helps individuals practice and become more proficient in using them.

Visual aids and social stories are valuable tools for helping individuals with ASD understand and regulate their emotions. For example, creating a visual chart of emotions with corresponding coping strategies can serve as a quick reference during emotional distress. Additionally, role-playing different scenarios can help individuals practice emotional responses in a controlled environment. Consistent practice and reinforcement of these strategies can enhance their effectiveness.

Structured environments and clear expectations also play a crucial role in emotional regulation. Establishing routine and providing predictable schedules can reduce anxiety and help individuals feel more secure. When individuals know what to expect, they are better equipped to manage their emotional responses. Creating a calm and organized space where they can retreat when feeling overwhelmed can further support emotional regulation.

IMPORTANCE OF ROUTINE AND STRUCTURE

Routine and structure are essential for individuals with ASD as they provide predictability and reduce anxiety. Establishing a daily routine helps individuals understand what to expect throughout the day, which can mitigate feelings of uncertainty and stress. Consistent schedules for activities such as meals, school, and bedtime help create a stable environment, making transitions between activities smoother and less distressing.

Visual schedules can be an effective tool in maintaining routine and structure. These schedules provide a clear and tangible representation of the day's activities, which can help individuals with ASD anticipate and prepare for upcoming events. Using visual timers and reminders can further support adherence to routines and make transitions more manageable.

Incorporating flexibility within a structured routine is also important. While consistency is key, allowing for some degree of flexibility can help individuals with ASD adapt to unexpected changes.

The gradual introduction of changes to the routine and providing advance notice can help reduce the stress associated with alterations, making it easier for individuals to adjust.

BUILDING RESILIENCE AND SELF-ESTEEM

Building resilience and self-esteem in individuals with ASD involves creating opportunities for success and fostering a positive self-image. Encouraging participation in activities where they can experience achievements and receive positive reinforcement helps build confidence. Celebrating small successes and providing constructive feedback supports their sense of accomplishment and boosts self-esteem.

Social skills training and positive peer interactions also play a significant role in developing resilience. By engaging in social activities and receiving support from peers, individuals with ASD can learn effective communication strategies and build relationships. This social engagement helps them feel connected and valued, contributing to a stronger sense of self-worth.

Promoting self-advocacy is another important aspect of building resilience. Encouraging individuals with ASD to express their needs and preferences helps them gain a sense of control over their lives. Providing them with tools and opportunities to advocate for themselves empowers them to navigate challenges with greater confidence and resilience.

ACCESSING MENTAL HEALTH SUPPORT AND RESOURCES

Accessing mental health support and resources is crucial for individuals with ASD and their families. Identifying qualified mental health professionals who specialize in ASD can provide tailored interventions and support.

These professionals can offer therapies, counseling, and medication management to address specific mental health needs and co-occurring conditions.

Local support groups and online communities can also be valuable resources. Connecting with others who have similar experiences provides emotional support and practical advice. Many communities offer resources such as workshops, seminars, and advocacy services that can help individuals with ASD and their families navigate mental health challenges.

Navigating healthcare systems and insurance coverage is an important aspect of accessing mental health resources. Understanding what services are available and how to obtain them can help families secure the necessary support. It's essential to be proactive in seeking out these resources and advocating for the needs of individuals with ASD to ensure they receive appropriate care and support.

CHAPTER EIGHT

NAVIGATING FAMILY DYNAMICS AND SUPPORT

IMPACT OF ASD ON FAMILY RELATIONSHIPS

Autism Spectrum Disorder (ASD) can profoundly affect family dynamics, often creating emotional and practical challenges that reshape family relationships. Parents may experience stress and anxiety as they navigate the complexities of their child's needs, which can strain their relationship with each other. The constant demands of caregiving can lead to feelings of isolation or resentment, disrupting the balance within the family unit. Siblings might also feel neglected or confused by the extra attention given to their sibling with ASD, leading to a range of emotional responses from guilt to frustration.

In addition, extended family members may struggle to understand the condition, leading to misunderstandings or lack of support. The diverse reactions within the family can create a fragmented environment, where consistent, supportive interactions become crucial. It's essential for family members to openly communicate their feelings and experiences to foster understanding and mitigate the stress that ASD may bring into their relationships.

To address these challenges, families need to establish routines and support structures that cater to everyone's needs. Implementing regular family meetings can provide a platform for sharing experiences and adjusting expectations. Families should consider seeking professional help if conflicts become overwhelming, ensuring that each member's perspective is heard and valued.

COPING STRATEGIES FOR PARENTS AND SIBLINGS

Parents and siblings of children with ASD often face unique challenges that require tailored coping strategies. For parents, it's vital to develop effective stress management techniques such as mindfulness, exercise, or engaging in hobbies. Establishing a support network through friends, family, or professional counselors can provide emotional relief and practical advice. Routine breaks and self-care are crucial for maintaining personal well-being and preventing burnout.

Siblings can benefit from strategies that help them understand and cope with their family situation. Educational resources tailored to their age can clarify their sibling's condition and reduce feelings of confusion. Encouraging open dialogue within the family allows siblings to express their feelings and concerns, which can foster empathy and strengthen their relationship with their sibling with ASD. Support groups specifically designed for siblings can offer valuable peer support and understanding.

Creating a balanced family environment involves setting aside time for each family member, including siblings, to engage in activities that they enjoy. Providing opportunities for individual attention and recognizing each member's contributions to the family can help maintain emotional balance and reduce feelings of neglect.

FINDING AND UTILIZING SUPPORT GROUPS

Support groups can be a vital resource for families affected by ASD, offering emotional support and practical advice from those with shared experiences. Finding a local or online support group involves researching community organizations, autism advocacy groups, and social media platforms. These groups often provide a range of resources, including workshops, informational sessions, and peer discussions, which can help families navigate the challenges of ASD.

Joining support groups allows families to connect with others facing similar struggles, providing a sense of community and understanding. These connections can lead to valuable insights into managing everyday challenges and accessing local resources such as therapy services or educational programs. Engaging with support groups also offers opportunities to learn about new coping strategies and interventions that may benefit their child with ASD.

It's important for families to actively participate in support groups and contribute their own experiences. Sharing personal stories can help others and foster a supportive environment where members can seek advice and offer support.

Ensuring that participation in these groups is consistent can provide ongoing benefits and reinforce a sense of community.

BALANCING CAREGIVING WITH PERSONAL WELL-BEING

Balancing caregiving responsibilities with personal well-being is essential for maintaining a healthy family dynamic. Caregivers must prioritize their health by scheduling regular breaks and engaging in activities that provide relaxation and joy.

Developing a structured routine that includes time for self-care helps prevent caregiver burnout and ensures they remain emotionally and physically equipped to support their child with ASD.

Utilizing respite care services or enlisting the help of trusted family members can provide caregivers with much-needed relief. Creating a support network that includes friends, family, and professional resources can offer practical assistance and emotional encouragement. By delegating tasks and sharing responsibilities, caregivers can manage their well-being more effectively.

Setting realistic goals and boundaries is also crucial for maintaining balance. Caregivers should recognize their limits and seek professional guidance when needed. Establishing a healthy balance between caregiving duties and personal time is key to sustaining long-term well-being and ensuring that all family members' needs are met.

STRENGTHENING FAMILY COMMUNICATION AND UNITY

Effective communication is central to fostering family unity and managing the impact of ASD. Regular family meetings can provide a platform for discussing concerns, celebrating successes, and planning together. Encouraging open dialogue helps family members express their feelings, share information about their experiences, and address any misunderstandings that may arise.

Implementing family activities that promote bonding can reinforce relationships and create positive experiences together. Activities such as family outings, shared hobbies, or even simple daily rituals can strengthen connections and provide opportunities for quality time. Consistent and empathetic communication helps in understanding each other's perspectives and reduces the potential for conflict.

Providing education about ASD to all family members can also improve communication and foster unity. Understanding the condition and its effects on behavior allows family members to respond more effectively and compassionately.

CHAPTER NINE

PLANNING FOR THE FUTURE

TRANSITIONING TO ADULTHOOD AND INDEPENDENT LIVING

Transitioning to adulthood for individuals with Autism Spectrum Disorder (ASD) involves careful preparation and structured planning. To facilitate a smooth transition, it is crucial to develop life skills that promote independence, such as managing daily routines, personal hygiene, and household responsibilities. Start by creating a personalized plan that includes goals for acquiring these skills, and integrate them into daily activities through consistent practice and positive reinforcement. This helps build confidence and ensures that the individual is well-prepared for living independently.

A supportive environment is essential during this transition. Engage with vocational rehabilitation services, community programs, and special education services that provide tailored support.

These services often offer training programs designed to develop essential skills and provide guidance on navigating adult responsibilities. Ensure that the individual has access to resources that address their specific needs and preferences, making the transition process more manageable and less overwhelming.

Additionally, fostering social skills and providing opportunities for meaningful social interactions can greatly aid in the transition. Social skills training programs and group activities can help individuals with ASD build and maintain relationships, which are crucial for emotional support and integration into the community. Creating a network of support that includes family, friends, and professionals can provide the necessary encouragement and assistance as they embark on this new phase of life.

EMPLOYMENT AND VOCATIONAL TRAINING OPPORTUNITIES

Employment and vocational training are vital components for individuals with ASD aiming to achieve economic independence and job satisfaction. Identifying suitable job opportunities starts with assessing the individual's interests, strengths, and challenges. Tailoring job searches to align with these personal attributes increases the likelihood of finding fulfilling employment. Work with career counselors or job coaches who specialize in ASD to develop a resume that highlights relevant skills and experiences.

Vocational training programs are available to help individuals with ASD gain the necessary skills for specific careers. These programs often include job readiness training, internships, and hands-on experiences in real work environments.

By participating in these programs, individuals can acquire practical skills, build work experience, and receive valuable feedback that helps them improve their job performance. Additionally, many programs offer support in job placement and ongoing career development.

Networking and community connections can also play a significant role in finding employment opportunities. Engage with local organizations and support groups that specialize in ASD and employment. These groups often have partnerships with employers and can provide referrals, job fairs, and networking events tailored to individuals with ASD. Building relationships within these communities can enhance job prospects and provide additional support throughout the employment journey.

FINANCIAL PLANNING AND LEGAL CONSIDERATIONS

Financial planning is a crucial aspect of ensuring long-term stability for individuals with ASD. Start by creating a comprehensive budget that includes all sources of income, such as disability benefits or part-time employment, and outlines essential expenses like housing, utilities, and healthcare. Working with a financial advisor who understands the specific needs of individuals with ASD can guide managing finances, setting financial goals, and making informed decisions.

Legal considerations are also important in financial planning. Understanding eligibility for government benefits, such as Supplemental Security Income (SSI) or Medicaid, and navigating the application process can significantly impact financial stability. Additionally, consider establishing a Special Needs Trust to ensure that financial assets are managed appropriately without jeopardizing eligibility for public assistance programs. Consulting with a legal professional specializing in disability law can help ensure compliance with legal requirements and optimize financial planning.

Estate planning is another critical aspect of financial planning. Create a plan that addresses long-term care needs, designates guardianship, and outlines the distribution of assets. Involving family members and legal professionals in this process ensures that the individual's wishes are documented and that their financial and care needs are addressed in the future.

Regularly review and update the plan to accommodate any changes in circumstances or legal requirements.

COMMUNITY RESOURCES AND SUPPORT SERVICES

Accessing community resources and support services is essential for individuals with ASD to thrive. Start by identifying local organizations that offer support tailored to the needs of individuals with ASD, such as support groups, advocacy organizations, and educational programs. These organizations often provide a range of services, including social activities, counseling, and educational workshops, which can enhance social skills and personal development.

Additionally, many communities have specialized programs designed to support individuals with ASD in areas such as healthcare, housing, and transportation. Connect with local agencies that offer these services to explore available options. Utilizing community resources can help address specific needs, provide valuable information, and connect individuals with additional support networks.

Engaging with online forums and national organizations can also be beneficial. These platforms offer access to a wealth of information, including resources, support groups, and advocacy opportunities. By participating in these online communities, individuals and families can gain insights, share experiences, and receive support from others who face similar challenges.

LONG-TERM GOALS AND LIFE PLANNING

Setting long-term goals and life planning is crucial for individuals with ASD to achieve a fulfilling and independent life. Start by establishing clear, achievable goals related to personal, educational, and vocational aspirations. Break these goals into smaller, manageable steps and create a timeline for reaching them. Regularly review and adjust the goals as needed to ensure they remain relevant and attainable.

Incorporate ongoing evaluation and adaptation into the life planning process. Periodically assess progress toward goals and make adjustments based on changes in circumstances, interests, or needs. This flexible approach helps accommodate evolving aspirations and challenges, ensuring that the life plan remains practical and aligned with the individual's personal growth.

Collaborate with professionals, family members, and support networks to develop a comprehensive life plan. Engage in regular discussions about progress, seek input from those involved, and utilize available resources to address any obstacles. A collaborative approach ensures that the plan is well-rounded and that the individual receives the necessary support to achieve their long-term goals.

CHAPTER TEN

COMMON CONCERNS

HOW DO I KNOW IF MY CHILD NEEDS A DIAGNOSIS?

Identifying whether your child may need a diagnosis of Autism Spectrum Disorder (ASD) often begins with observing developmental milestones and behavioral patterns. Early signs include difficulties with communication, such as limited speech or nonverbal cues, as well as challenges with social interactions, like difficulty making eye contact or forming relationships. Repetitive behaviors, such as hand-flapping or intense focus on specific objects, can also be indicators. Keeping detailed records of these behaviors and developmental concerns will help provide a clearer picture for health professionals.

Consulting with a pediatrician or child psychologist is a crucial step if you suspect your child may need a diagnosis. These professionals can conduct developmental screenings and refer you to specialists for a comprehensive evaluation. The diagnostic process often involves a combination of observational assessments, standardized tests, and interviews with you about your child's behavior and developmental history. Seeking a formal assessment can help determine whether your child meets the criteria for an ASD diagnosis and guide appropriate interventions.

In addition to professional evaluations, gathering feedback from your child's school and other caregivers can provide valuable insights. Teachers and daycare providers can offer observations on social interactions and classroom behavior that may be indicative of ASD.

Collecting information from various sources ensures a more comprehensive understanding of your child's needs and helps in making an informed decision about pursuing a formal diagnosis.

WHAT SHOULD I DO IF I DISAGREE WITH A PROFESSIONAL'S ASSESSMENT?

If you find yourself disagreeing with a professional's assessment of your child, the first step is to seek clarification on their findings and the rationale behind their conclusions. Request a detailed explanation of the diagnostic process, the criteria used, and how the assessment was conducted. Understanding the basis for their evaluation can provide insight into whether your concerns have been fully addressed or if additional information is needed.

Consider seeking a second opinion from another qualified specialist if you remain unconvinced by the initial assessment. Different professionals may use varied diagnostic approaches or have different perspectives, which can offer a more comprehensive view of your child's condition. Ensure that the second opinion is from a reputable expert in ASD, and provide them with all relevant information from the initial assessment to facilitate an accurate evaluation.

Additionally, open communication with the initial professional is key. Discuss your concerns and provide any new observations or evidence that might influence the diagnosis. Collaborative discussions can sometimes lead to a re-evaluation or adjustment of the initial assessment, ensuring that the diagnosis and subsequent recommendations accurately reflect your child's needs.

HOW CAN I EFFECTIVELY COMMUNICATE MY CHILD'S NEEDS TO TEACHERS AND THERAPISTS?

Effectively communicating your child's needs to teachers and therapists involves providing clear, detailed information about your child's strengths, challenges, and specific requirements. Prepare a written summary that outlines key aspects of your child's behavior, sensory sensitivities, communication style, and any strategies that have been successful in managing their needs. This summary will serve as a useful reference for teachers and therapists to tailor their approaches to your child's unique needs.

Regular, open communication with educators and therapists is essential for ensuring that your child's needs are understood and met. Schedule meetings or regular check-ins to discuss your child's progress, address any concerns, and adjust strategies as needed. Active collaboration helps in creating a consistent support system across different environments, which is crucial for your child's development and well-being.

Encourage teachers and therapists to provide feedback on your child's progress and any challenges they observe. This reciprocal communication helps in making informed decisions about interventions and adjustments. Being proactive in sharing updates from home and listening to professional insights can lead to more effective support for your child.

WHAT ARE THE BEST WAYS TO SUPPORT MY CHILD DURING THERAPY SESSIONS?

Supporting your child during therapy sessions involves creating a positive, encouraging environment that reinforces the goals of the therapy. Attend sessions regularly, if possible, to understand the techniques and strategies being used and to provide consistency between home and therapy settings. Positive reinforcement and encouragement during sessions can help your child feel more comfortable and motivated.

Collaborate closely with the therapist to understand the objectives of each session and the specific skills or behaviors being targeted. Implementing suggested strategies at home can reinforce the work done during therapy and help your child generalize new skills across different contexts. Consistency and practice outside of therapy sessions are crucial for achieving progress.

Be patient and flexible as therapy can be challenging for both your child and you. Celebrate small successes and be prepared for setbacks. Maintaining a supportive and understanding attitude helps create a nurturing environment that fosters your child's growth and makes therapy a more positive experience.

HOW CAN I MANAGE THE STRESS AND EMOTIONAL IMPACT OF CARING FOR A CHILD WITH ASD?

Managing the stress of caring for a child with Autism Spectrum Disorder involves developing a strong support network. Connect with support groups, both online and in-person, where you can share experiences and gain advice from others in similar situations. These connections can provide emotional support and practical strategies for dealing with challenges.

Incorporate self-care practices into your routine to maintain your well-being. Regular exercise, adequate rest, and engaging in hobbies can help alleviate stress and improve your overall mood. Finding time for yourself, even if it's just a few minutes a day, is crucial for preventing burnout and maintaining the energy needed to support your child effectively.

Consider seeking professional counseling or therapy if the emotional impact becomes overwhelming. Mental health professionals can provide coping strategies, stress management techniques, and a safe space to process your feelings. Addressing your own emotional needs ensures that you are better equipped to support your child and navigate the demands of caregiving.